Don't be afraid to be Saints

World Youth Days 1984-2008

John Paul II
&
Benedict XVI

All booklets are published thanks to the generous support of the members of the Catholic Truth Society

CATHOLIC TRUTH SOCIETY
PUBLISHERS TO THE HOLY SEE

As I look at you now, at your young faces, at your genuine enthusiasm, from the depths of my heart I want to give thanks to God for the gift of youth, which continues to be present in the Church and in the world because of you. Thank God for the World Youth Days! Thanks be to God for all the young people who have been involved in them in the past sixteen years! Many of them are now adults who continue to live their faith in their homes and workplaces. I am sure, dear friends, that you too will be as good as those who preceded you. You will carry the proclamation of Christ into the new millennium. When you return home, do not grow lax. Reinforce and deepen your bond with the Christian communities to which you belong. From Rome, from the City of Peter and Paul, the Pope follows you with affection and, paraphrasing Saint Catherine of Siena's words[1], reminds you: "If you are what you should be, you will set the whole world ablaze!"[2]

Pope John Paul II

- Come to Sydney -

My dear young friends, I hope to see very many of you in Sydney in July 2008.[3] It will be a providential opportunity to experience the fullness of the Holy Spirit's power. Come in great numbers in order to be a sign of hope and to give appreciative support to the Church community in Australia that is preparing to welcome you. For the young people of the country that will host you, it will be an exceptional opportunity to proclaim the beauty and joy of the Gospel to a society that is secularised in so many ways. Australia, like all of Oceania, needs to rediscover its Christian roots. ... I invite you to give time to prayer and to your spiritual formation during this last stage of the journey leading to the 23rd World Youth Day, so that in Sydney you will be able to renew the promises made at your Baptism and Confirmation. Together we shall invoke the Holy Spirit, confidently asking God for the gift of a new Pentecost for the Church and for humanity in the third millennium.[4]

Pope Benedict XVI

Contents

Come to Sydney 3

Christ is your Teacher 5

Discover your Vocation 13

Become a Witness 23

Formed by the Eucharist and Sacraments 29

Born to Love and Serve 39

The Challenge: Christ or the World? 51

To Live the Truth 61

Pilgrims looking for Christ 70

- Christ is your Teacher -

Mary and the Cross

Christ's call leads along a way which is not easy to travel, because it can also lead us to the Cross. But there is no other way which leads to truth and which can give life. Nevertheless, we are not alone on this path. Mary, through her *fiat*, opened a new way for humanity. By her acceptance of, and total dedication to the mission of her Son, she is the prototype of every Christian vocation. She will walk with us, she will be our travelling companion, and with her help we will be capable of following the vocation which Christ offers us. Dear young people, let us set out upon our way with Mary; let us commit ourselves to following Christ, the Way, Truth and Life. Thus we will be zealous bearers of the message of the new evangelisation and generous builders of the civilisation of love.[5]

Teach us to love

Good Shepherd, teach the young people gathered here, teach the young people of the world, the meaning of "laying down" their lives through vocation and mission. Just as you sent the Apostles to preach the Gospel to the ends of the earth, so now challenge the youth of the Church to carry on the vast mission of making you known to all those who have not yet heard of you! Give these young people the courage and generosity of the great missionaries of the past so that, through the witness of their faith and their solidarity with every brother and sister in need, the world may discover the Truth, the Goodness and the Beauty of the Life you alone can give.

Teach the young people gathered here to take your message of life and truth, of love and solidarity, to the heart of the modern metropolis - to the heart of all the problems which afflict the human family at the end of the twentieth century. Teach these young people the proper use of their freedom. Teach them that the greatest freedom is the fullest giving of themselves. Teach them the meaning of the Gospel words: "He who loses his life for my sake will find it" (*Mt* 10:39).[6]

Resurrection stronger than death

The victory of life over death is what every human being desires. All religions, especially the great religious traditions followed by most of the peoples of Asia, bear witness to how deeply the truth regarding our immortality is inscribed in man's religious consciousness. Man's search for life after death finds definitive fulfilment in the Resurrection of Christ. Because the Risen Christ is the demonstration of God's response to this deeply-felt longing of the human spirit, the Church professes: "I believe in the resurrection of the body and in life everlasting" (*Symbolum Apostolorum*). The Risen Christ assures the men and women of every age that they are called to a life beyond the frontier of death.[7]

Who can fulfill our deepest longings?

Dear young people, if we are here today, it is because we identify with the Apostle Peter's reply: "Lord, to whom shall we go? You have the words of eternal life" (*Jn* 6:68).

Around you, you hear all kinds of words. But only Christ speaks words that stand the test of time and remain for all eternity. The time of life that you are living calls for decisive choices on your part: decisions about the direction of your studies, about work, about your role in society and in the Church. It is important to realise that among the many questions surfacing in your minds, the decisive ones are not about "what". The basic question is "who": "who" am I to go to, "who" am I to follow, "to whom" should I entrust my life?

You are thinking about love and the choices it entails, and I imagine that you agree: what is really important in life is the choice of the person who will share it with you. But be careful! Every human person has inevitable limits: even in the most successful of marriages there is always a certain amount of disappointment. So then, dear friends, does not this confirm what we heard the Apostle Peter say? Every human being finds himself sooner or later saying what he said: "To whom shall we go? You have the words of eternal life". Only Jesus of Nazareth, the Son of God and of Mary, the eternal Word of the Father born two thousand years ago at Bethlehem in Judaea, is capable of satisfying the deepest aspirations of the human heart. ... And it is possible to meet the divine Master personally: he is in fact truly present on the altar in the reality of his Body and Blood. In the Eucharistic Sacrifice, we can enter into contact with the person of Jesus in a way that is mysterious but real, drinking at the inexhaustible fountain that is his life as the Risen Lord.[8]

Stake your lives on Christ

You are young, and the Pope is old, 82 or 83 years of life is not the same as 22 or 23. But the Pope still fully identifies with your hopes and aspirations. Although I have lived through much darkness, under harsh totalitarian regimes, I have seen enough evidence to be unshakably convinced that no difficulty, no fear is so great that it can completely suffocate the hope that springs eternal in the hearts of the young. You are our hope, the young are our hope.

Do not let that hope die! Stake your lives on it! We are not the sum of our weaknesses and failures; we are the sum of the Father's love for us and our real capacity to become the image of his Son.

I finish with a prayer. O Lord Jesus Christ, keep these young people in your love. Let them hear your voice and believe what you say, for you alone have the words of life. Teach them how to profess their faith, bestow their love, and impart their hope to others. Make them convincing witnesses to your Gospel in a world so much in need of your saving grace. Make them the new people of the Beatitudes, that they may be the salt of the earth and the light of the world at the beginning of the Third Christian Millennium![9]

Jesus gives meaning to our lives

This evening I will give you the Gospel. It is the Pope's gift to you at this unforgettable vigil. The word which it contains is the word of Jesus. If you listen to it in silence, in prayer, seeking help in understanding what it means for your life from the wise counsel of your priests and teachers, then you will meet Christ and you will follow him, spending your lives day by day for him! It is Jesus in fact that you seek when you dream of happiness; he is waiting for you when nothing else you find satisfies you; he is the beauty to which you are so attracted; it is he who provokes you with that thirst for fullness that will not let you settle for compromise; it is he who urges you to shed the masks of a false life; it is he who reads in your hearts your most genuine choices, the choices that others try to stifle. It is Jesus who stirs in you the desire to do something great with your lives, the will to follow an ideal, the refusal to allow yourselves to be grounded down by mediocrity, the courage to commit yourselves humbly and patiently to improving yourselves and society, making the world more human and more fraternal.

Dear young people, in these noble undertakings you are not alone. With you there are your families, there are your communities, there are your priests and teachers, there are so many of you who in the depths of your hearts never weary of loving Christ and believing in him. In the struggle against sin you are not alone: so many like you are struggling and through the Lord's grace are winning![10]

The fruits of Jesus in us

Christ must be evident in our lives. It must be seen in our capacity to forgive. It must be seen in our sensitivity to the needs of others. It must be seen in our willingness to share. It must be seen in our commitment to our neighbours, both those close at hand and those physically far away, whom we nevertheless consider to be close. Today, there are many forms of voluntary assistance, models of mutual service, of which our society has urgent need. We must not, for example, abandon the elderly to their solitude, we must not pass by when we meet people who are suffering. If we think and live according to our communion with Christ, then our eyes will be opened. Then we will no longer be content to scrape a living just for ourselves, but we will see where and how we are needed.

Living and acting thus, we will soon realise that it is much better to be useful and at the disposal of others than to be concerned only with the comforts that are offered to us.

I know that you as young people have great aspirations, that you want to pledge yourselves to build a better world. Let others see this, let the world see it, since this is exactly the witness that the world expects from the disciples of Jesus Christ; in this way, and through your love above all, the world will be able to discover the star that we follow as believers. Let us go forward with Christ and let us live our lives as true worshippers of God![11]

The Holy Spirit is teacher of the interior life

My dear young friends, the Holy Spirit continues today to act with power in the Church, and the fruits of the Spirit are abundant in the measure in which we are ready to open up to this power that makes all things new. For this reason it is important that each one of us know the Spirit, establish a relationship with Him and allow ourselves to be guided by Him. However, at this point a question naturally arises: who is the Holy Spirit for me? It is a fact that for many Christians He is still the "great unknown". This is why, as we prepare for the next World Youth Day, I wanted to invite you to come to know the Holy Spirit more deeply at a personal level. In our profession of faith we proclaim: "I believe in the Holy Spirit, the Lord and giver of life, who proceeds from the Father and the Son" (Nicene-Constantinopolitan Creed). Yes, the Holy Spirit, the Spirit of the love of the Father and of the Son, is the Source of life that makes us holy, "because God's love has been poured into our hearts through the Holy Spirit which has been given to us" (*Rm* 5:5). Nevertheless, it is not enough to know the Spirit; we must welcome Him as the guide of our souls, as the "Teacher of the interior life" who introduces us to the Mystery of the Trinity, because He alone can open us up to faith and allow us to live it each day to the full. The Spirit impels us forward towards others, enkindles in us the fire of love, makes us missionaries of God's charity.

I know very well that you young people hold in your hearts great appreciation and love for Jesus, and that you desire to meet Him and speak with Him. Indeed, remember that it is precisely the presence of the Spirit within us that confirms, constitutes and builds our person on the very Person of Jesus crucified and risen. So let us become familiar with the Holy Spirit in order to be familiar with Jesus.[12]

- Discover your Vocation -

What does Jesus want of me?

You have come full of hopeful anticipation and confidence, setting aside the snares of the world, truly to meet Jesus, "the Way, the Truth and the Life", who has invited each one of you to follow him lovingly. This is a universal call, which does not take the colour of one's skin into account, nor one's social condition or age. On this night, so moving for its religious significance, fraternity and youthful joy, Christ, as Friend, is in the midst of the Assembly to ask you personally if you want to follow decidedly the way which he is showing you, if you are prepared to accept his truth, his message of salvation, if you want to live the Christian ideal fully. It is a decision which you must take without fear. God will help you; he will give you his light and his strength so that you may respond generously to his call, a call to a total Christian life. Respond to the call of Jesus Christ and follow him![13]

Your vocation in Christ

Jesus went in search of the men and women of his time. He engaged them in an open and truthful dialogue, whatever their condition. As the Good Samaritan of the human family, he came close to people to heal them of their sins and of the wounds which life inflicts, and to bring them back to the Father's house. Young people of "World Youth Day", the Church asks you to go, in the power of the Holy Spirit, to those who are near and those who are far away. Share with them the freedom you have found in Christ. People thirst for genuine inner freedom. They yearn for the Life which Christ came to give in abundance. The world at the approach of a new millennium, for which the whole Church is preparing, is like a field ready for the harvest. Christ needs labourers ready to work in his vineyard. May you, the Catholic young people of the world, not fail him. In your hands, carry the Cross of Christ. On your lips, the words of Life. In your hearts, the saving grace of the Lord.[14]

Purpose of your life

You ask, "what are my expectations of young people?". In *Crossing the Threshold of Hope* I have written that "the fundamental problem of youth is profoundly personal. Young people... know that their life has meaning to the extent that it becomes a free gift for others" (John Paul II, *Crossing the Threshold of Hope*, p. 121). A question therefore is directed to each one of you personally: are you capable of giving of yourself, your time, your energies, your talents, for the good of others? Are you capable of love? If you are, the Church and society can expect great things from each one of you.

The vocation to love, understood as true openness to our fellow human beings and solidarity with them, is the most basic of all vocations. It is the origin of all vocations in life. That is what Jesus was looking for in the young man when he said: "Keep the commandments" (cf. *Mk* 10:19). In other words: "Serve God and your neighbour according to all the demands of a true and upright heart". And when the young man indicated that he was already following that path, Jesus invited him to an even greater love: "Leave all and come, follow me: leave everything that concerns only yourself and join me in the immense task of saving the world" (cf. *ibid.*, 10:21). Along the path of each person's existence, the Lord has something for each one to do.[15]

Vocation to marriage

Christ's call is not addressed only to the Brothers, Sisters and priests. He calls everyone; he also calls those who, upheld by love, want to get married. It is God, in fact, who created the human being male and female, thus introducing into history that singular duality thanks to which man and woman, although essentially having equal rights, have the characteristic of that wonderful complementary of attributes, which brings about mutual attraction. The love which blossoms when masculinity and femininity meet embodies the call of God himself, who created man "in his image and likeness", precisely as "man and woman". Christ has made this call his own, and enriched it with new values in the definitive Covenant established on the Cross. So, my dear friends, in the love of every baptised person, he asks to be able to express his love for the Church, for which he sacrificed himself so "that he might present the Church to himself in splendour, without spot or wrinkle or any such thing, that she might be holy and without blemish" (*Ep* 5:27). Christ wishes to teach you the wonderful wealth of nuptial love. Let him speak to your hearts. Do not run away from him. He has something important to tell you for the future of your love. Above all with the grace of the sacrament, he has something decisive to give you, so that your love will have the necessary strength to overcome the trials of life.[16]

Discover your true vocation

As the Successor of Peter, I too have come to invite you to ask Christ: "Where are you staying?". If you ask him this question sincerely, you will be able to hear his response and receive from him the courage and strength to carry it out. The question is born of a quest. Men and women seek God. Young people realise in the depths of their being that this quest is the inner law of their lives. Human beings seek their way in the visible world and, through the visible world, they seek the unseen world at every stage of their spiritual journey. Each of us can repeat the words of the

Psalmist: "Your face, Lord, do I seek; hide not your face from me" (*Ps* 27:8-9). We all have our personal history and an innate desire to see God, a desire which makes itself felt at the same time as we discover the created world. This world is wonderful and rich; it sets before us countless treasures; it enchants us; it attracts both our reason and our will. But in the end it does not satisfy our spirit. Man realises that this world, with all its many riches, is superficial and precarious; in a sense, it is destined for death. Nowadays, we are more aware of the fragility of our earth, too often degraded by the hand of man himself, to whom the Creator entrusted it.

As regards man himself, each person comes into the world, is born from a mother's womb, grows and matures. We discover our vocation and develop our personality throughout our years of activity; then the moment comes when we must leave this world. The longer we live, the more we realise how precarious life is, and the more we wonder about immortality: what exists beyond the frontiers of death? Then, from the depths of our being, there arises the same question asked of the one who conquered death: "Rabbi, where are you staying?". Teacher, you who love and respect the human person, you who have shared in human suffering, you who illumine the mystery of human existence, help us to discover the true meaning of our life and vocation! "Your face, Lord, do I seek; hide not your face from me" (*Ps* 27:8-9).[17]

Marriage and family

But, more than one of you is asking himself or herself: What does Jesus want of me? To what is he calling me? What is the meaning of his call for me? For the great majority of you, human love will present itself as a way of self-realisation in the formation of a family. This is why, in the name of Christ I want to ask you: Are you prepared to follow the call of Christ through the Sacrament of Marriage, so as to be procreators of new life, people who will form new pilgrims to the heavenly city?

In the history of salvation, Christian marriage is a mystery of faith. The family is a mystery of love, because it collaborates directly in the creative work of God. Beloved young people, a large sector of society does not accept Christ's teachings, and, consequently, it takes other roads: hedonism, divorce, abortion, birth control and contraceptive methods. These ways of understanding life are in clear contrast to the Law of God and the teachings of the Church. To follow Christ faithfully means putting the Gospel message into practice, and this also implies chastity, the defence of life, and also the indissolubility of the matrimonial bond, which is not a mere contract which can be arbitrarily broken.

Living in the "permissiveness" of the modern world, which denies or minimises the authenticity of Christian principles, it is easy and attractive to breathe in this contaminated mentality and give in to the passing desire. But, bear in mind that those who act in this way neither follow Christ nor love him. To love means to walk together in the same direction towards God, who is the Source of Love. In this Christian framework, love is stronger than death because it prepares us to welcome life, to protect it and defend it from the mother's womb until death.[18]

To defend love

Are you prepared to protect human life with the maximum care at every moment, even in the most difficult ones? Are you prepared, as young Christians, to live and defend love through indissoluble marriage, to protect the stability of the family, a stability which favours the balanced upbringing of children, under the protection of a paternal and maternal love, which complement each another?

This is the Christian witness that is expected of the majority of you, young men and women. To be a Christian means to be a witness to Christian truth, and today, particularly, it is to put into practice the authentic meaning which Christ and the Church give to life and to the full realisation of young men and women through marriage and the family.[19]

Become builders of a new era

The aspiration that humanity nurtures, amid countless injustices and sufferings, is the hope of a new civilisation marked by freedom and peace. But for such an undertaking, a new generation of builders is needed. Moved not by fear or violence but by the urgency of genuine love, they must learn to build, brick by brick, the city of God within the city of man. Allow me, dear young people, to consign this hope of mine to you: you must be those "builders"! You are the men and women of tomorrow. The future is in your hearts and in your hands. God is entrusting to you the task, at once difficult and uplifting, of working with him in the building of the civilisation of love. If your friendship with Christ, your knowledge of his mystery, your giving of yourselves to him, are genuine and deep, you will be "children of the light", and you will become "the light of the world". For this reason I repeat to you the Gospel words: "Let your light so shine before others, that they may see your good works and give glory to your Father who is in heaven" (*Mt* 5:16).[20]

Christ's challenge

Young pilgrims, Christ needs you to enlighten the world and to show it the "path to life" (*Ps* 16, 11). The challenge is to make the Church's "yes" to Life concrete and effective. The struggle will be long, and it needs each one of you. Place your intelligence, your talents, your enthusiasm, your compassion and your fortitude at the service of life! Have no fear. The outcome of the battle for

Life is already decided, even though the struggle goes on against great odds and with much suffering. This certainty is what the Second Reading declares: "Christ is now raised from the dead, the first fruits of those who have fallen asleep. ...so in Christ all will come to life again" (1 *Co* 15, 20-22). The paradox of the Christian message is this: Christ - the Head - has already conquered sin and death. Christ in his Body - the pilgrim People of God - continually suffers the onslaught of the Evil One and all the evil which sinful humanity is capable of.[21]

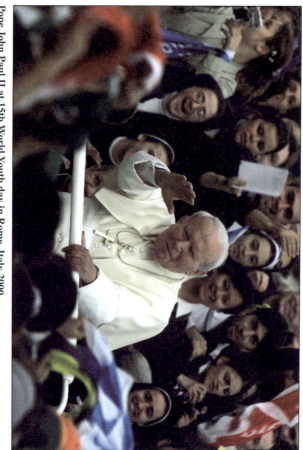

Pope John Paul II at 15th World Youth day in Rome, Italy, 2000.

- Become a Witness -

To be witnesses

What does it mean to give witness to Christ? It simply means to live in accordance with the Gospel: "You shall love the Lord your God with all your heart, with all your soul, and with all your mind... You shall love your neighbour as yourself" (*Mt* 22:37, 39). The Christian is called to serve his neighbour and society, to promote and support the dignity of every human being, to respect, defend and favour the right of the person, to be a builder of a lasting and authentic peace based on fraternity, freedom, justice and truth. Despite the marvellous possibilities which modern technology offers man, there is still a great deal of poverty and misery in the world. In many parts of the world people live menaced by violence, by terrorism and even by war. ... It is urgently necessary to be able to count on envoys of Christ, on Christian messengers. And you, young people, young men and young women, in the future you will be these envoys or messengers.[22]

What Christ expects of you

And so we come back to your original question: what does the Church and the Pope expect of the young people? That you confess Jesus Christ. And that you learn to proclaim all that the message of Christ contains for the true liberation and genuine progress of humanity. This is what Christ expects of you. This is what the Church looks for in the young people of the Philippines, of Asia, of the world. In this way your own cultures will find that you speak a language which is already echoed in some way in the ancient traditions of Asia: the language of true interior peace and the fullness of life, now and for ever.[23]

Being sent

Sons and daughters ... To each one of you Christ says: "I am sending you". Why is he sending you? Because men and women the world over - north, south, east and west - long for true liberation and fulfilment. The poor seek justice and solidarity; the oppressed demand freedom and dignity; the blind cry out for light and truth (cf. *Lk* 4:18). You are not being sent to proclaim some abstract truth. The Gospel is not a theory or an ideology! The Gospel is life! Your task is to bear witness to this life: the life of God's adopted sons and daughters. Modern man, whether he knows it or not, urgently needs that life - just as two thousand years ago humanity was in need of Christ's coming; just as people will always need Jesus Christ until the end of time.[24]

The glorious Cross: witnesses

With his remarkable fervour, Saint Paul repeats: "We preach Christ Crucified". He whom the world considered as nothing but weakness and folly is the one whom we proclaim as Power and Wisdom, the fulness of Truth. It is true that our confidence has its highs and lows. Certainly our vision of faith is often darkened by doubt and by our own weakness. Humble and poor sinners that we are, let us accept the message of the Cross. In order to answer our question: "Rabbi, where are you staying?", Christ summons us: come and see; in the Cross you will see the radiant sign of the world's redemption, the loving presence of the living God. Because Christians realise that the Cross dominates history, they place the crucifix in their churches and along roadsides, or they wear it near their hearts. For the Cross is a genuine sign of the presence of the Son of God; by this sign he is revealed as the Redeemer of the world.[25]

Living as Christians

It is in the midst of your brothers and sisters that you are to live as Christians. In Baptism God has given us a mother, the Church, with whom we grow spiritually in order that we may walk the path of holiness. This sacrament incorporates you as members of a people, it makes you sharers in the life of the Church and gives you brothers and sisters to love, in order that you might be "one in Christ" (*Ga* 3:28). In the Church, no longer are there borders; we are one people standing together, made up of many groups with different cultures, attitudes and modes of behaviour, in communion with the Bishops, the pastors of the flock. This unity is a sign of richness and vitality. In diversity, your first concern must be for unity and fraternal cohesion, which will enable personal development to take place in a serene way and allow the whole body to grow.[26]

You are the morning watchmen

Dear friends, at the dawn of the Third Millennium I see in you the "morning watchmen" (cf. *Is* 21:11-12). In the course of the century now past young people like you were summoned to huge gatherings to learn the ways of hatred; they were sent to fight against one another. The various godless messianic systems which tried to take the place of Christian hope have shown themselves to be truly horrendous. Today you have come together to declare that in the new century you will not let yourselves be made into tools of violence and destruction; you will defend peace, paying the price in your person if need be. You will not resign yourselves to a world where other human beings die of hunger, remain illiterate and have no work. You will defend life at every moment of its development; you will strive with all your strength to make this earth ever more livable for all people. Dear young people of the century now beginning, in saying "yes" to Christ, you say "yes" to all your noblest ideals. I pray that he will reign in your hearts and in all of humanity in the new century and the new millennium. Have no fear of entrusting yourselves to him! He will guide you, he will grant you the strength to follow him every day and in every situation. May Mary most holy, the Virgin who said "yes" to God throughout her whole life, may Saints Peter and Paul and all the Saints who have lighted the Church's journey down the ages, keep you always faithful to this holy resolve![27]

The world needs witnesses

The "spirit of the world" offers many false illusions and parodies of happiness. There is perhaps no darkness deeper than the darkness that enters young people's souls when false prophets extinguish in them the light of faith and hope and love. The greatest deception, and the deepest source of unhappiness, is the illusion of finding life by excluding God, of finding freedom by excluding moral truths and personal responsibility. The Lord is calling you to choose between these two voices competing for your souls. That decision is the substance and challenge of World Youth Day. Why have you come together from all parts of the world? To say in your hearts: "Lord, to whom shall we go?" Who has the words of eternal life? "You have the words of eternal life" (*Jn* 6, 68). Jesus - the intimate friend of every young person - has the words of life. The world you are inheriting is a world which desperately needs a new sense of brotherhood and human solidarity. It is a world which needs to be touched and healed by the beauty and richness of God's love. It needs witnesses to that love. The world needs salt. It needs you - to be the salt of the earth and the light of the world.

Salt is used to preserve and keep. As apostles for the Third Millennium, your task is to preserve and keep alive the awareness of the presence of our Saviour Jesus Christ, especially in the celebration of the Eucharist, the memorial of his saving death and glorious resurrection. You must keep alive the memory of the words of life which he spoke, the marvellous works of mercy and goodness which he performed. You must constantly remind the world of the "power of the Gospel to save" (*Rm* 1, 16)!

Salt seasons and improves the flavour of food. Following Jesus, you have to change and improve the "taste" of human history. With your faith, hope and love, with your intelligence, courage and perseverance, you have to humanise the world we live in, in the way that today's Reading from Isaiah indicates: "loose the bonds of injustice ... share your bread with the hungry ... remove the pointing of the finger, the speaking of evil.... Then your light shall rise in the darkness" (*Is* 58, 6-10).[28]

- Formed by the Eucharist and Sacraments -

Your baptism

Dear young people, do you know what the sacrament of Baptism does to you? God acknowledges you as his children and transforms your existence into a story of love with him. He conforms you to Christ so that you will be able to fulfil your personal vocation. He has come to make a pact with you and he offers you his peace. Live from now on as children of the light who know that they are reconciled by the Cross of the Saviour! ... As baptised individuals, you bear witness to Christ by your concern for a life that is upright and faithful to the Lord, maintained by means of a spiritual and moral struggle. Faith and moral behaviour are linked. In fact, the gift received leads us to a permanent conversion, so that we might imitate Christ and be worthy of the divine promise. The word of God transforms the lives of those who accept it, because it is the rule of faith and action. In their lives, in order to respect fundamental values, Christians also experience that suffering which can result from moral choices opposed to worldly behaviour and which therefore can be heroic. But this is the price of the life of blessed happiness with the Lord. Dear young people, this is the price of your witness. I count on your courage and fidelity.[29]

Confirmation

You might ask, how can we allow ourselves to be renewed by the Holy Spirit and to grow in our spiritual lives? The answer, as you know, is this: we can do so by means of the Sacraments, because faith is born and is strengthened within us through the Sacraments, particularly those of Christian initiation: Baptism, Confirmation and the Eucharist ...This truth concerning the three Sacraments that initiate our lives as Christians is perhaps neglected in the faith life of many Christians. They view them as events that took place in the past and have no real significance for today, like roots that lack life-giving nourishment. It happens that many young people distance themselves from their life of faith after they have received Confirmation. There are also young people who have not even received this sacrament. Yet it is through the sacraments of Baptism, Confirmation and then, in an ongoing way, the Eucharist, that the Holy Spirit makes us children of the Father, brothers and sisters of Jesus, members of his Church, capable of a true witness to the Gospel, and able to savour the joy of faith.

Confirmation gives us special strength to witness to and glorify God with our whole lives (cf. *Rm* 12:1). It makes us intimately aware of our belonging to the Church, the "Body of Christ", of which we are all living members, in solidarity with one another (cf. 1 *Co* 12:12-25). By allowing themselves to be guided by the Spirit, each baptised person can bring his or her own contribution to the building up of the Church because of the charisms given by the Spirit, for "to each is given the manifestation of the Spirit for the common good" (1 *Co* 12:7). When the Spirit acts, he brings his fruits to the soul, namely "love, joy, peace, patience, kindness, generosity, faithfulness, gentleness, and self-control" (*Ga* 5:22). To those of you who have not yet received the sacrament of Confirmation, I extend a cordial invitation to prepare to receive it, and to seek help from your priests. It is a special occasion of grace that the Lord is offering you. Do not miss this opportunity![30]

Eucharist

"Rabbi, where are you staying?" Each day the Church responds: Christ is present in the Eucharist, in the sacrament of his death and resurrection. In and through the Eucharist, you acknowledge the dwelling-place of the living God in human history. For the Eucharist is the sacrament of the love which conquers death; it is the sacrament of the Covenant, pure gift of love for the reconciliation of all humanity. It is the gift of the real presence of Jesus the Redeemer, in the bread which is his body given up for us, in the wine which is his blood poured out for all. Thanks to the Eucharist, constantly renewed among all the peoples of the world, Christ continues to build his Church: he brings us together in praise and thanksgiving for salvation, in the communion which only infinite love can forge. Our worldwide gathering now takes on its fullest meaning, through the celebration of Mass. Dear young friends, may your presence here mean a true commitment in faith! For Christ is now answering your own question and the questions of all those who seek the living God. He answers by offering an invitation: this is my Body, take it and eat. To the Father he entrusts his supreme desire: that all those whom he loves may be one in the same communion.[31]

The love of Jesus

The Eucharist is the sacrament of the presence of Christ, who gives himself to us because he loves us. He loves each one of us in a unique and personal way in our practical daily lives: in our families, among our friends, at study and work, in rest and relaxation. He loves us when he fills our days with freshness, and also when, in times of suffering, he allows trials to weigh upon us: even in the most severe trials, he lets us hear his voice. Yes, dear friends, Christ loves us and he loves us for ever! He loves us even when we disappoint him, when we fail to meet his expectations for us. He never fails to embrace us in his mercy. How can we not be grateful to this God who has redeemed us, going so far as to accept the foolishness of the Cross? To God who has come to be at our side and has stayed with us to the end?[32]

The world needs to see our love

To celebrate the Eucharist, "to eat his flesh and drink his blood", means to accept the wisdom of the Cross and the path of service. It means that we signal our willingness to sacrifice ourselves for others, as Christ has done. Our society desperately needs this sign, and young people need it even more so, tempted as they often are by the illusion of an easy and comfortable life, by drugs and pleasure-seeking, only to find themselves in a spiral of despair, meaninglessness and violence. It is urgent to change direction and to turn to Christ. This is the way of justice, solidarity and commitment to building a society and a future worthy of the human person. This is our Eucharist, this is the answer that Christ wants from us, from you young people at the closing of your Jubilee. Jesus is no lover of half measures, and he does not hesitate to pursue us with the question: "Will you also go away?" In the presence of Christ, the Bread of Life, we too want to say today with Peter: "Lord, to whom shall we go? You have the words of eternal life" (*Jn* 6:68).[33]

The Eucharist makes witnesses

Dear friends, when you go back home, set the Eucharist at the centre of your personal life and community life: love the Eucharist, adore the Eucharist and celebrate it, especially on Sundays, the Lord's Day. Live the Eucharist by testifying to God's love for every person. I entrust to you, dear friends, this greatest of God's gifts to us who are pilgrims on the paths of time, but who bear in our hearts a thirst for eternity. May every community always have a priest to celebrate the Eucharist! I ask the Lord therefore to raise up from among you many holy vocations to the priesthood. Today as always the Church needs those who celebrate the Eucharistic Sacrifice with a pure heart. The world must not be deprived of the gentle and liberating presence of Christ living in the Eucharist!

You yourselves must be fervent witnesses to Christ's presence on the altar. Let the Eucharist mould your life and the life of the families you will form. Let it guide all life's choices. May the Eucharist, the true and living presence of the love of the Trinity, inspire in you ideals of solidarity, and may it lead you to live in communion with your brothers and sisters in every part of the world. In a special way, may sharing in the Eucharist lead to a new flourishing of vocations to the religious life. In this way the Church will have fresh and generous energies for the great task of the new evangelisation. If any of you, dear young men and women, hear the Lord's inner call to give yourselves completely to him in order to love him "with an undivided heart" (cf. 1 *Co* 7:34), do not be held back by doubts or fears. Say "yes" with courage and without reserve, trusting him who is faithful to his promises. Did he not assure those who had left everything for his sake that they would have a hundredfold in this life and eternal life hereafter? (cf. *Mk* 10:29-30).[34]

What Jesus has done for us in the Eucharist

At the celebration of the Eucharist, we find ourselves in the "hour" of Jesus, to use the language of John's Gospel. Through the Eucharist this "hour" of Jesus becomes our own hour, his presence in our midst. Together with the disciples he celebrated the Passover of Israel, the memorial of God's liberating action that led Israel from slavery to freedom. Jesus follows the rites of Israel. He recites over the bread the prayer of praise and blessing. But then something new happens. He thanks God not only for the great works of the past; he thanks him for his own exaltation, soon to be accomplished through the Cross and Resurrection, and he speaks to the disciples in words that sum up the whole of the Law and the Prophets: "This is my Body, given in sacrifice for you. This cup is the New Covenant in my Blood". He then distributes the bread and the cup, and instructs them to repeat his words and actions of that moment over and over again in his memory.

What is happening? How can Jesus distribute his Body and his Blood? By making the bread into his Body and the wine into his Blood, he anticipates his death, he accepts it in his heart, and he transforms it into an action of love. What on the outside is simply brutal violence - the

Crucifixion - from within becomes an act of total self-giving love. This is the substantial transformation which was accomplished at the Last Supper and was destined to set in motion a series of transformations leading ultimately to the transformation of the world when God will be all in all (cf. 1 *Co* 15:28). In their hearts, people always and everywhere have somehow expected a change, a transformation of the world. Here now is the central act of transformation that alone can truly renew the world: violence is transformed into love, and death into life. Since this act transmutes death into love, death as such is already conquered from within, the Resurrection is already present in it. Death is, so to speak, mortally wounded, so that it can no longer have the last word.

To use an image well known to us today, this is like inducing nuclear fission in the very heart of being - the victory of love over hatred, the victory of love over death. Only this intimate explosion of good conquering evil can then trigger off the series of transformations that little by little will change the world. All other changes remain superficial and cannot save. For this reason we speak of redemption: what had to happen at the most intimate level has indeed happened, and we can enter into its dynamic. Jesus can distribute his Body, because he truly gives himself. This first fundamental transformation of violence into love, of death into life, brings other changes in its wake. Bread and wine become his Body and Blood.

But it must not stop there; on the contrary, the process of transformation must now gather momentum. The Body and Blood of Christ are given to us so that we ourselves will be transformed in our turn. We are to become the Body of Christ, his own Flesh and Blood. We all eat the one bread, and this means that we ourselves become one. In this way, adoration, as we said earlier, becomes union. God no longer simply stands before us as the One who is totally Other. He is within us, and we are in him. His dynamic enters into us and then seeks to spread outwards to others until it fills the world, so that his love can truly become the dominant measure of the world.[35]

Love the Mass: it changes your life

Sometimes, our initial impression is that having to include time for Mass on a Sunday is rather inconvenient. But if you make the effort, you will realise that this is what gives a proper focus to your free time. Do not be deterred from taking part in Sunday Mass, and help others to discover it too. This is because the Eucharist releases the joy that we need so much, and we must learn to grasp it ever more deeply, we must learn to love it. Let us pledge ourselves to do this - it is worth the effort! Let us discover the intimate riches of the Church's liturgy and its true greatness: it is not we who are celebrating for ourselves, but it is the living God himself who is preparing a banquet for us.[36]

Nourished by Christ

In order to grow in our Christian life, we need to be nourished by the Body and Blood of Christ. In fact, we are baptised and confirmed with a view to the Eucharist ...The Eucharist is a "perpetual Pentecost" since every time we celebrate Mass we receive the Holy Spirit who unites us more deeply with Christ and transforms us into Him. My dear young friends, if you take part frequently in the eucharistic celebration, if you dedicate some of your time to adoration of the Blessed Sacrament, the Source of love which is the Eucharist, you will acquire that joyful determination to dedicate your lives to following the Gospel. At the same time it will be your experience that whenever our strength is not enough, it is the Holy Spirit who transforms us, filling us with his strength and making us witnesses suffused by the missionary fervour of the risen Christ.[37]

- Born to Love and Serve -

To love and to serve

Why are you here, you young people of the nineties and of the twentieth century? Do you feel perchance within yourselves "the spirit of this world"? Have you not perhaps come here - I ask you again - to convince yourselves once and for all that to be great means to serve? This service is certainly not mere humanitarian sentimentality. Nor is the community of the disciples of Christ a volunteer agency or social help group. Such a concept of service would imply stooping to the level of the "spirit of this world". No! Here we are dealing with something more. The radicality, quality and destiny of this "service" to which we have all been called must be seen in the context of the human Redemption. Because we have been created, we have been called, we have been destined, first and foremost, to serve God, in the image and likeness of Christ who, as Lord of all creation, as centre of the cosmos and of history, showed his royal power through obedience unto death, and was glorified in the Resurrection (cf. *Lumen Gentium*, 36). The kingdom of God is realised by means of this "service", which is the fullness and measure of all human service. It does not act according to human criterion through power, might and money. Each one of us is asked for a total readiness to follow Christ, who "came not to be served, but to serve".[38]

To grow in true freedom

I invite you, dear friends, to discover your true vocation to cooperate in the spreading of this Kingdom of truth and life, of holiness and grace, of justice, love and peace. If you really wish to serve your brothers and sisters, let Christ reign in your hearts, let him help you to discern and grow in dominion over yourselves, to strengthen you in the virtues, to fill you above all with his charity, to guide you along the path which leads to the "condition of the perfect one". Do not be afraid to be saints! This is the liberty with which Christ has set us free (cf. *Ga* 5:1). Not as the powers of this world promise it, with false hope and deceit: total autonomy, a breaking of every dependency as creatures and sons and daughters, an affirmation of self-sufficiency which leaves us defenceless before our limitations and weaknesses, alone in the prison of our egoism, slaves to the "spirit of this world", condemned to the "bondage of decay" (*Rm* 8:21). For this reason, I ask the Lord, to help you to grow in this "true freedom", as a basic and illuminating criterion of judgement and choice in life. This same freedom will direct your moral behaviour in truth and in charity. It will help you to discover authentic love, uncorrupted by an alienating and harmful permissiveness. It will make you people who are open to a possible total self-giving in the priesthood or consecrated life. It will make you grow in humanness through study and work. It will inspire your works of solidarity and your acts of service to those in need, whether in body or in soul. It will enable you to become "masters", so as to serve better, and not "slaves", victims and followers of the dominant trends in attitudes and ways of behaviour.[39]

A new martyrdom

To believe in Jesus today, to follow Jesus as Peter, Thomas, and the first Apostles and witnesses did, demands of us, just as it did in the past, that we take a stand for him, almost to the point at times of a new martyrdom: the martyrdom of those who, today as yesterday, are called to go against the tide in order to follow the divine Master, to follow "the Lamb wherever he goes" (*Rv* 14:4). It is not by chance, dear young people, that I wanted the witnesses to the faith in the twentieth century to be remembered at the Colosseum during this Holy Year. Perhaps you will not have to shed your blood, but you will certainly be asked to be faithful to Christ! A faithfulness to be lived in the circumstances of everyday life: I am thinking of how difficult it is in today's world for engaged couples to be faithful to purity before marriage. I think of how the mutual fidelity of young married couples is put to the test. I think of friendships and how easily the temptation to be disloyal creeps in. I think also of how those who have chosen the path of special consecration have to struggle to persevere in their dedication to God and to their brothers and sisters. I think of those who want to live a life of solidarity and love in a world where the only things that seem to matter are the logic of profit and one's personal or group interest.[40]

To serve: to be a person for others

Yes! You need to know well the gifts God has granted you in Christ. It is necessary to know well the gift you have received, in order to give it to others, to contribute to the common good. Yes. You need to perceive well the gifts God has granted you in Christ. You need to know well the gift you have received in the very experience of family and parish life, in working together with others in associations, and in the charismatic flourishing of movements, so as to be able to give it to others: thus to enrich the communion and missionary thrust of the Church, to be witnesses of Christ in your neighbourhood and school, in the university and factory, in places of work and recreation..., to contribute to the common good, as servants of experiences of growth in humanity, of dignity and solidarity, in which young people may be authentic protagonists of more human ways of life.[41]

Love Christ and each other

This is what the Apostle teaches. What he says is not just a mere teaching, but a fervent call.

"Let love be genuine; hate what is evil, hold fast to what is good; love one another with brotherly affection; outdo one another in showing honour. Never flag in zeal, be aglow with the Spirit, serve the Lord. Rejoice in your hope, be patient in tribulation, be constant in prayer. Contribute to the needs of the saints, practise hospitality" (*Rm* 12:9-13). Is he not perhaps saying this particularly to you, to young people? Does the fact that you are young not imply a particular sensitivity to this plan of life and action, to this world of values? Does it not open towards this world? And if, by chance, it feels the resistance which comes from within, or indeed from without, does not your being young dispose you to struggle precisely for just such a "form" of life? This form has been given to human life by Christ. He knows what is within man (cfr. *Jn* 2:25). "Christ the new Adam, in the very revelation of the mystery of the Father and of his love, fully reveals man to himself and brings to light his most high calling" (*Gaudium et Spes*, 22). Dear young people, let yourselves be won by him! Christ alone is the way, the truth and the life as, in the remarkable Gospel synthesis, the theme of our World Youth Day proclaims.[42]

The need and urgency of mission

Many young people view their lives with apprehension and raise many questions about their future. They anxiously ask: How can we fit into a world marked by so

Pope Benedict XVI at 20th World Youth day in Cologne, Germany 2005.

many grave injustices and so much suffering? How should we react to the selfishness and violence that sometimes seem to prevail? How can we give full meaning to life? How can we help to bring it about that the fruits of the Spirit mentioned above, "love, joy, peace, patience, kindness, generosity, faithfulness, gentleness, and self-control" can fill this scarred and fragile world, the world of young people most of all? On what conditions can the life-giving Spirit of the first creation and particularly of the second creation or redemption become the new soul of humanity? Let us not forget that the greater the gift of God - and the gift of the Spirit of Jesus is the greatest of all - so much the greater is the world's need to receive it and therefore the greater and the more exciting is the Church's mission to bear credible witness to it.[43]

Mission to love

You young people, through World Youth Day, are in a way manifesting your desire to participate in this mission. In this regard, my dear young friends, I want to remind you here of some key truths on which to meditate. Once again I repeat that only Christ can fulfil the most intimate aspirations that are in the heart of each person. Only Christ can humanise humanity and lead it to its "divinisation". Through the power of his Spirit he instils divine charity within us, and this makes us capable of loving our neighbour and ready to be of service. The Holy Spirit enlightens us, revealing Christ crucified and risen, and shows us how to become more like Him so that we can be "the image and instrument of the love which flows from Christ" (*Deus Caritas Est*, 33). Those who allow themselves to be led by the Spirit understand that placing oneself at the service of the Gospel is not an optional extra, because they are aware of the urgency of transmitting this Good News to others. Nevertheless, we need to be reminded again that we can be witnesses of Christ only if we allow ourselves to be led by the Holy Spirit who is "the principal agent of evangelisation" (cf. *Evangelii Nuntiandi*, 75) and "the principal agent of mission" (cf. *Redemptoris Missio*, 21).[44]

Bearers of the good news

Moreover, two thousand years ago twelve Apostles gave their lives to make Christ known and loved. Throughout the centuries since then, the Gospel has continued to spread by means of men and women inspired by that same missionary fervour. Today too there is a need for disciples of Christ who give unstintingly of their time and energy to serve the Gospel. There is a need for young people who will allow God's love to burn within them and who will respond generously to his urgent call, just as many young blesseds and saints did in the past and also in more recent times. In particular, I assure you that the

Spirit of Jesus today is inviting you young people to be bearers of the good news of Jesus to your contemporaries. The difficulty that adults undoubtedly find in approaching the sphere of youth in a comprehensible and convincing way could be a sign with which the Spirit is urging you young people to take this task upon yourselves. You know the ideals, the language, and also the wounds, the expectations, and at the same time the desire for goodness felt by your contemporaries. This opens up the vast world of young people's emotions, work, education, expectations, and suffering ... Each one of you must have the courage to promise the Holy Spirit that you will bring one young person to Jesus Christ in the way you consider best, knowing how to "give an explanation to anyone who asks you for a reason for your hope, but [to] do it with gentleness and reverence" (cf. 1 *P* 3:15).[45]

Be holy missionaries

In order to achieve this goal, my dear friends, you must be holy and you must be missionaries since we can never separate holiness from mission (cf. *Redemptoris Missio*, 90). Do not be afraid to become holy missionaries like Saint Francis Xavier who travelled through the Far East proclaiming the Good News until every ounce of his strength was used up, or like Saint Thérèse of the Child Jesus who was a missionary even though she never left the Carmelite convent. Both of these are "Patrons of the

Missions". Be prepared to put your life on the line in order to enlighten the world with the truth of Christ; to respond with love to hatred and disregard for life; to proclaim the hope of the risen Christ in every corner of the earth.⁴⁶

The Church needs you

At this stage of history, the liberating message of the Gospel of Life has been put into your hands. And the mission of proclaiming it to the ends of the earth is now passing to your generation. Like the great Apostle Paul, you too must feel the full urgency of the task: "Woe to me if I do not evangelise" (1 *Co* 9, 16). Woe to you if you do not succeed in defending life. The Church needs your energies, your enthusiasm, your youthful ideals, in order to make the Gospel of Life penetrate the fabric of society, transforming people's hearts and the structures of society in order to create a civilisation of true justice and love. Now more than ever, in a world that is often without light and without the courage of noble ideals, people need the fresh, vital spirituality of the Gospel. Do not be afraid to go out on the streets and into public places, like the first Apostles who preached Christ and the Good News of salvation in the squares of cities, towns and villages. This is no time to be ashamed of the Gospel (cf. *Rm* 1, 16). It is the time to preach it from the rooftops (cf. *Mt* 10, 27). Do not be afraid to break out of comfortable and routine modes of living, in order to take up the challenge of making Christ known in the modern "metropolis". It is you who must "go out into the byroads" (*Mt* 22, 9) and invite everyone you meet to the banquet which God has prepared for his people. The Gospel must not be kept hidden because of fear or indifference. It was never meant to be hidden away in private. It has to be put on a stand so that people may see its light and give praise to our heavenly Father.[47]

Your mission

How does Jesus send you? He promises neither sword nor money nor power, nor any of the things which the means of social communications make attractive to people today. He gives you instead grace and truth. He sends you out with the powerful message of his Paschal Mystery, with the truth of his Cross and Resurrection. That is all he gives you, and that is all you need. This grace and truth will in turn give rise to courage. Following Christ has always demanded courage. The Apostles, the martyrs, entire generations of missionaries, saints and confessors - known and unknown, and in every part of the world - have had the strength to stand firm in the face of misunderstanding and adversity. ... Christians have paid the price of their fidelity and that is the sure source of the Church's confidence.[48]

- The Challenge: Christ or the World? -

Christ or the world

Young people have come in pilgrimage to the tomb of the Apostle to learn that Gospel truth: "whoever would be great among you must be your servant". In these words we find the essential criterion of human greatness. This criterion is new. It was new in the time of Christ and continues to be so two thousand years later. This criterion is new. It implies a transformation, a renewal of the criteria by which the world is governed. "You know that the rulers of the Gentiles lord it over them, and their great men exercise authority over them. It shall not be so among you" (*Mt* 20:25-26). The criterion by which the world is governed is the criterion of success. To have power ... To have economic power, so as to make the dependence of others be seen. To have cultural power in order to manipulate consciences. To use ... and to abuse! Such is the "spirit of this world". Does this mean perhaps that power in itself is evil? Does this mean that the economy - economic initiative - is in itself bad?

No! By no means. Both of them can also be a way of serving. This is the spirit of Christ, the truth of the Gospel. This truth and this spirit are expressed in the Cathedral of Santiago de Compostela through the Apostle, who - according to his mother's wish - would be the first; however - following Christ - he became a servant.[49]

What are you looking for?

Why are you here, you young people of the nineties and of the twentieth century? Do you feel perhaps within yourselves "the spirit of this world", in so far as this era, rich in means of use and abuse, struggles against the spirit of the Gospel? Have you not perhaps come here to convince yourselves once and for all that to be great means to serve? However... are you prepared to drink of this cup? Are you prepared to let yourselves be permeated by the body and blood of Christ; so as to die to the old man which is in us and rise again with him? Do you feel the Lord's strength which can enable you to bear your sacrifices, sufferings and the "crosses" which weigh upon the young people who are disoriented as regards the meaning of life, manipulated by power, unemployed, hungry, submerged in drugs and violence, slaves of the eroticism which is spreading everywhere...? Know that Christ's yoke is easy... and that only in him will we find the hundredfold here and now, and eternal life later.[50]

What the world offers

Today, many voices around you speak a language different from that of Christ, proposing models of behaviour which, in the name of a "modernity" freed from "complexes" and "taboos" - as it is the custom to say - reduce love to a fleeting experience of personal satisfaction or even of mere sexual enjoyment. To those who are able to look at this type of relationship without prejudice, it is not difficult to distinguish behind the loud words the disappointing reality of egoistic behaviour, which aims principally at a personal advantage. The other is no longer accepted as a subject with his or her dignity, but is degraded to the level of an object, disposed of not according to the criteria of values but of interests. Even the child, who should be the living fruit of the love of his parents, which incarnates, in a way transcends, and perpetuates itself in him, ends up by being considered a thing which one has the right to accept or reject according to one's state of mind. How can one fail to notice the woodworm of a consumer mentality that has slowly emptied love of its exceptional content, in which is manifested the spark of the fire which burns in the heart of the Holy Trinity. One must bring love back to its eternal source if one wants it to give real gratification, joy, life. To you young people falls the duty of being witnesses in the world of today to the truth of love. It is a demanding reality which often contrasts with current opinions and "slogans". But it is the only truth worthy of human beings called to form part of the family of God![51]

What is the meaning of life?

Dear young people, Christ is the Life. I am sure that each of you loves life, not death. You wish to live life to the full, animated by hope arising from a far-reaching plan. It is right that you have a thirst for life, for a full life. You are young precisely for this. However, in what does life consist? What is the meaning of life, and what is the best way of realising it? A short time ago you sang with enthusiasm: *Somos peregrinos de la vida, caminantes unidos para amar*, (We are pilgrims in this life, travelling together in order to love). Is not this the clue to the answer you are seeking? The Christian faith places a deep link between love and life. In John's Gospel we read: "God so loved the world that he gave his only Son, that whoever believes in him should not perish but have eternal life" (*Jn* 3:16). God's love brings us to life, and this love and life are realised in Jesus Christ. He is the Incarnate Love of the Father; in him "the goodness and loving kindness of God our Saviour appeared" (*Tt* 3:4).

Dear young people, Christ is therefore the one competent interlocutor to whom you can put the essential questions about the value and meaning of life, not only a healthy, happy life, but also a life weighed down by suffering, whether marked by some physical disability or by difficult family and social conditions. Yes, even for tragic problems which can be expressed more by groans than by words, Christ is the competent interlocutor. Ask him, listen to him! The meaning of life. He will say to you: keep loving. Only the person who forgets self in order to give himself to others fulfils his own life and expresses to the greatest extent the value of his earthly existence. It is the evangelic paradox of the life which is redeemed by being lost (cf. *Jn* 12:25), a paradox which finds its full explanation in the mystery of Christ who died and rose for us. Dear young people, the mature perspective of a human and Christian vocation is presented to us as part of the gift. This is important above all in the case of a religious vocation, by which a man or a woman, through the profession of the evangelical counsels, takes on for the sake of the Kingdom of God the programme which Christ himself carried out on earth. Religious commit themselves to give a particular witness, placing the love of God above all other things, and remind everyone of the common call to union with God in eternity. The world of today needs these witnesses now as never before, because very frequently it is so occupied with the things of this earth that it forgets those of heaven.[52]

Choices: good and evil

Why do the consciences of young people not rebel against this situation, especially against the moral evil which flows from personal choices? Why do so many acquiesce in attitudes and behaviour which offend human dignity and disfigure the image of God in us? The normal thing would be for conscience to point out the mortal danger to the individual and to humanity contained in the easy acceptance of evil and sin. And yet, it is not always so. Is it because conscience itself is losing the ability to distinguish good from evil? In a technological culture in which people are used to dominating matter, discovering its laws and mechanisms in order to transform it according to their wishes, the danger arises of also wanting to manipulate conscience and its demands. In a culture which holds that no universally valid truths are possible, nothing is absolute. Therefore, in the end - they say - objective goodness and evil no longer really matter. Good comes to mean what is pleasing or useful at a particular moment. Evil means what contradicts our subjective wishes. Each person can build a private system of values.[53]

Stick to your conscience

Young people, do not give in to this widespread false morality. Do not stifle your conscience! Conscience is the most secret core and sanctuary of a person, where we are alone with God (cf. *Gaudium et Spes*, 16). "In the depths of his conscience man detects a law which he does not impose upon himself, but which holds him to obedience" (cf. *Gaudium et Spes*, 16). That law is not an external human law, but the voice of God, calling us to free ourselves from the grip of evil desires and sin, and stimulating us to seek what is good and true. Only by listening to the voice of God in your most intimate being, and by acting in accordance with its directions, will you reach the freedom you yearn for. As Jesus said, only the truth will make you free (cf. *Jn* 8:32). And the truth is not the fruit of each individual's imagination. God gave you intelligence to know the truth, and your will to achieve what is morally good. He has given you the light of conscience to guide your moral decisions, to love good and avoid evil. Moral truth is objective, and a properly formed conscience can perceive it. But if conscience itself has been corrupted, how can it be restored? If conscience - which is light - no longer enlightens, how can we overcome the moral darkness? Jesus says: "The eye is the body's lamp. If your eyes are good, your body will be filled with light; if your eyes are bad, your body will be in darkness. And if your light is darkness, how deep will the darkness be!" (*Mt* 6:22-23). But Jesus also says: "I am the light of the world. No follower of mine shall ever walk in darkness; no, he shall possess the light of life" (*Jn* 8:12). If you follow Christ you will restore conscience to its rightful place and proper role, and you will be the light of the world, the salt of the earth (cf. *Mt* 5:13). A re-birth of conscience must come from two sources: first, the effort to know objective truth with certainty, including the truth about God; and secondly, the light of faith in Jesus Christ, who alone has the words of Life.[54]

The world of our times

This marvelous world - so loved by the Father that he sent his only Son for its salvation (cf. *Jn* 3:17) - is the theater of a never-ending battle being waged for our dignity and identity as free, spiritual beings. This struggle parallels the apocalyptic combat described in the First Reading of this Mass. Death battles against Life: a "culture of death" seeks to impose itself on our desire to live, and live to the full. There are those who reject the light of life, preferring "the fruitless works of darkness" (*Ep* 5:11). Their harvest is injustice, discrimination, exploitation, deceit, violence. In every age, a measure of their apparent success is the death of the Innocents. In our own century, as at no other time in history, the "culture of death" has assumed a social and institutional form of legality to justify the most horrible crimes against humanity: genocide, "final solutions", "ethnic cleansings", and the massive "taking of lives of human beings even before they are born, or before they reach the natural point of death" (*Dominum et Vivificantem*, 57). The Book of Revelation presents the Woman surrounded by hostile forces. The absolute nature of their attack is symbolised in the object of their evil intention: the Child, the symbol of new life. The "dragon" (*Rv* 12:3), the "ruler of this world" (*Jn* 12:31) and the "father of lies" (*Jn* 8:44), relentlessly tries to eradicate from human hearts the sense of gratitude and respect for the original, extraordinary and fundamental gift of God: human life itself. Today that struggle has become increasingly direct.[55]

Why we need Jesus

Why do we need him? Because Christ reveals the truth about man and man's life and destiny. He shows us our place before God, as creatures and sinners, as redeemed through his own Death and Resurrection, as making our pilgrim way to the Father's house. He teaches the fundamental commandment of love of God and love of neighbour. He insists that there cannot be justice, brotherhood, peace and solidarity without the Ten Commandments of the Covenant, revealed to Moses on Mount Sinai and confirmed by the Lord on the Mount of the Beatitudes (cf. *Mt* 5:3-12) and in his dialogue with the young man (cf. *ibid.*, 19:16-22). The truth about man - which the modern world finds so hard to understand - is that we are made in the image and likeness of God himself (cf. *Jn* 1:27), and precisely in this fact, apart from any other consideration, lies the inalienable dignity of every human being, without exception, from the moment of conception until natural death. But what is even more difficult for contemporary culture to understand is that this dignity, already forged in the creative act of God, is raised immeasurably higher in the mystery of the Incarnation of the Son of God. This is the message which you have to proclaim to the modern world: especially to the least fortunate, to the homeless and dispossessed, to the sick, the outcasts, to those who suffer at the hands of others. To each one you must say: Look to Jesus Christ in order to see who you really are in the eyes of God![56]

Tough age to live in

It is true that young people today experience difficulties that previous generations experienced only partially and in a limited way. The weakness of much of family life, the lack of communication between parents and children, the isolating and alienating influence of a large part of the media, all these things can produce confusion in young people about the truths and values which give a genuine meaning to life. False teachers, many belonging to an intellectual elite in the worlds of science, culture and the media, present an anti-Gospel. They declare that every ideal is dead, contributing in this way to the profound moral crisis affecting society, a crisis which has opened the way for the toleration and even exaltation of forms of behavior which the moral conscience and common sense formerly held in abhorrence. When you ask them: what must I do?, their only certainty is that there is no definite truth, no sure path. They want you to be like them: doubtful and cynical. Consciously or not, they advocate an approach to life that has led millions of young people into a sad loneliness in which they are deprived of reasons for hope and are incapable of real love.[57]

- To Live the Truth -

Pilgrims, what do you seek?

Let us reflect now on the meaning of the word "way", so that this conversion of heart and meeting with the Lord, which we are now experiencing, may give new meaning to our lives.

The word "way" is very closely related to the idea of "search". This aspect has been highlighted in the representation which we are seeing. What do you seek, pilgrims? the crossroads have asked. This crossroads represents the question which man puts to himself regarding the meaning of life, regarding the goal he wants to reach, regarding the reason for his behaviour. We have seen represented, in a very expressive manner, some of the things which frequently many people set up as the goal of their life and their activity: money, success, egoism, comfort. However, the young pilgrims in the play have seen that in the long term these do not satisfy man. These things are unable to fill the human heart.

What do you seek, pilgrims? Each one of us here must ask himself this question. But you above all, since you have your life ahead of you. I invite you to decide definitively the direction of your way.

With the very words of Christ, I ask you: "What do you seek?" (*Jn* 1:38). Do you seek God?

The spiritual tradition of Christianity not only underlines the importance of our search for God. It highlights something more important still: it is God who looks for us. He comes out to meet us.

Our way to Compostela means wanting to give an answer to our needs, to our questions, to our search; it also means going out to meet God who looks for us with a love so great that we can understand it only with difficulty.[58]

Where is the truth?

"We are seeking truth". The words of the last song must resound in our hearts, because they give the deepest meaning to St James's way: seek truth and proclaim it. Where is truth? "What is truth?" (*Jn* 18:38). Before you, someone else had already asked Jesus this question. During the stage performance, we were witnesses to the three answers that the world gives to these questions. The first: use all one's fervour for the instant gratification of one's senses, a constant search for the pleasures of life. To that the pilgrims replied: "We had fun, but ... we keep on walking in a vacuum". The second answer, that of the violent who are interested in having power and dominating others, was not accepted by pilgrims of the second scene either. This answer brings on not only the destruction of the dignity of another person - brother or sister - but also one's self-destruction. Certain experiences during this century, which are still going on today, demonstrate what the results are when one's goal is power and supremacy over others. The third answer, given by drug addicts, is the search for the liberation and the fulfilment of a person by escaping from reality. It is the sad experience of many persons, amongst them many young people of your ages, who have taken this road or other similar ones. Instead of guiding them towards freedom, these roads lead them to slavery and even self-destruction.[59]

See and face the true problems

I am sure that, like almost all young people of today, you are worried about air and sea pollution, and that the problem of ecology upsets you. You are shocked by the misuse made of the earth's products and the progressive destruction of the environment. And you are right. One must take a coordinated and responsible action before our planet suffers irreversible damage. But, dear young people, there exists also a pollution of ideas and morals which can lead to the destruction of man. The pollution is sin, from which lies are born. Truth and sin. We must admit that very often lies are presented to us with the features of truth. We must, therefore, use our judgement in recognising truth, the Word that comes from God, and repulse the temptations which come from the "Father of lies". I wish to speak about the sin of denying God, refusing the light. As it is written in the Gospel according to St John, "the true light" was in the world: the Word, "the world was made through him, yet the world knew him not" (cf. *Jn* 1:9, 10). "Therefore at the root of human sin is the lie which is a radical rejection of the truth contained in the Word of the Father, through whom is expressed the loving omnipotence of the Creator; the omnipotence and also the love 'of God the Father, Creator of heaven and earth'" (*Dominum et Vivificantem*, n. 33).[60]

Christ challenges you

You know how easy it is to avoid the fundamental questions. But your presence here shows that you will not hide from reality and from responsibility! You care about the gift of life that God has given you. You have confidence in Christ when he says: "I came that they may have life, and have it abundantly" (*Jn* 10:10). Our Vigil begins with an act of trust in the words of the Good Shepherd. In Jesus Christ, the Father expresses the whole truth concerning creation. We believe that in the life, death and Resurrection of Jesus the Father reveals all his love for humanity. That is why Christ calls himself "the sheepgate" (*Jn* 10:7). As the gate, he stands guard over the creatures entrusted to him. He leads them to the good pastures: "I am the gate. Whoever enters through me will be safe. He will go in and out, and find pasture" (*Jn* 10:9). As we reflect together on the Life which Jesus gives, I ask you to have the courage to commit yourselves to the truth.

Have the courage to believe the Good News about Life which Jesus teaches in the Gospel. Open your minds and hearts to the beauty of all that God has made and to his special, personal love for each one of you. Young people of the world, hear his voice!

Hear his voice and follow him! Only the Good Shepherd will lead you to the full truth about Life.[61]

Defend life and give life

"I am the good shepherd. The good shepherd lays down his life for the sheep" (*Jn* 10:11). Our first reflection is inspired by these words of Jesus in the Gospel of Saint John. The Good Shepherd lays down his life. Death assails Life. At the level of our human experience, death is the enemy of life. It is an intruder who frustrates our natural desire to live. This is especially obvious in the case of untimely or violent death, and most of all in the case of the killing of the innocent. It is not surprising then that among the Ten Commandments the Lord of Life, the God of the Covenant, should have said on Mount Sinai "You shall not kill" (*Ex* 20:13; cf. *Mt* 5:21). The words "you shall not kill" were engraved on the tablets of the Covenant - on the stone tablets of the Law. But, even before that, this law was engraved on, the human heart, in the sanctuary of every individual's conscience. In the Bible, the first to experience the force of this law was Cain, who murdered his brother Abel. Immediately after his terrible crime, he felt the whole weight of having broken the commandment not to kill. Even though he tried to escape from the truth, saying: "Am I my brother's keeper?" (*Gn* 4:9), the inner voice repeated over and over: "You are a murderer". The voice was his conscience, and it could not be silenced.[62]

Search for the truth

In your questions I see repeated once more the scene from the Gospel, where a young man asks Jesus: Good Teacher, what must I do (cf. *Mk* 10:17)? The first thing that Jesus looked for was the attitude behind the question, the sincerity of the search. Jesus understood that the young man was sincerely looking for the truth about life and about his own personal path in life. This is important. Life is a gift of a certain period of time in which each one of us faces a challenge which life itself brings: the challenge of having a purpose, a destiny, and of striving for it. The opposite is to spend our lives on the surface of things, to "lose" our lives in futility; never to discover in ourselves the capacity for good and for real solidarity, and therefore never to discover the path to true happiness. Too many young people do not realise that they themselves are the ones who are mainly responsible for giving a worthwhile meaning to their lives. The mystery of human freedom is at the heart of the great adventure of living life well.[63]

True religion and meaning of life

In vast areas of the world today there is a strange forgetfulness of God. It seems as if everything would be just the same even without him. But at the same time there is a feeling of frustration, a sense of dissatisfaction with everyone and everything. People tend to exclaim: "This cannot be what life is about!". Indeed not. And so, together with forgetfulness of God there is a kind of new explosion of religion. I have no wish to discredit all the manifestations of this phenomenon. There may be sincere joy in the discovery. But to tell the truth, religion often becomes almost a consumer product. People choose what they like, and some are even able to make a profit from it. But religion sought on a "do-it-yourself" basis cannot ultimately help us. It may be comfortable, but at times of crisis we are left to ourselves. Help people to discover the true star which points out the way to us: Jesus Christ! Let us seek to know him better and better, so as to be able to guide others to him with conviction.[64]

Where is the truth for now and the future?

The question that arises is dramatic: on what foundations must we build the new historical era that is emerging from the great transformations of the twentieth century? Is it enough to rely on the technological revolution now taking place, which seems to respond only to criteria of productivity and efficiency, without reference to the individual's spiritual dimension or to any universally shared ethical values? Is it right to be content with provisional answers to the ultimate questions, and to abandon life to the impulses of instinct, to short-lived sensations or passing fads? The question will not go away: on what foundations, on what certainties should we build our lives and the life of the community to which we belong? Dear Friends, spontaneously in your hearts, in the enthusiasm of your young years you know the answer, and you are saying it through your presence here this evening: Christ alone is the cornerstone on which it is possible solidly to build one's existence. Only Christ - known, contemplated and loved - is the faithful friend who never lets us down, who becomes our travelling companion, and whose words warm our hearts (cf. *Lk* 24:13-35). The twentieth century often tried to do without that cornerstone, and attempted to build the city of man without reference to Him. It ended by actually building that city against man! Christians know that it is not possible to reject or ignore God without demeaning man.[65]

Nothing human is hurt by the gospel

This evening the Pope, along with all of you, young people from every continent, reaffirms before the world the faith that sustains the life of the Church. Christ is the light of the nations. He died and rose again in order to give back to those who journey through time the hope of eternity. Nothing human is hurt by the Gospel: every authentic value, in whatever culture it appears, is accepted and raised up by Christ. Knowing this, Christians cannot fail to feel in their hearts the pride and responsibility of their call to be witnesses to the light of the Gospel. Precisely for this reason I say to you this evening: let the light of Christ shine in your lives! Do not wait until you are older in order to set out on the path of holiness! Holiness is always youthful, just as eternal is the youthfulness of God. Communicate to everyone the beauty of the contact with God that gives meaning to your lives. In the quest for justice, in the promotion of peace, in your commitment to brotherhood and solidarity, let no one surpass you![66]

- Pilgrims looking for Christ -

You have come here on pilgrimage to. You have come to find your personal vocation. You draw close to the altar to offer, with the bread and wine, your youth, your search for truth, and everything which is good and beautiful in you. All that creative restlessness. All the sufferings of your young hearts. Being here among you, I wish to say with the Psalmist: Behold "the earth has yielded its harvest" (*Ps* 67[66]:6), its most precious fruit: the person, human youth. May the Face of God reflected in the human face of Christ. Redeemer of man, shine before you. "Let the peoples praise thee, O God; let all the peoples praise thee" (*Ps* 67[66]:5). May your contemporaries, contemplating your pilgrimage, be able to exclaim: "Let us go with you, for we have heard that God is with you" (*Zc* 8:23). This is the wish of the Pope, the Bishop of Rome, who has participated with you in this pilgrimage.[67]

The journey does not end here

Dear young people, your journey does not end here. Time does not come to a halt. Go forth now along the roads of the world, along the pathways of humanity, while remaining ever united in Christ's Church! Continue to contemplate God's glory and God's love, and you will receive the enlightenment needed to build the civilisation of love, to help our brothers and sisters to see the world transfigured by God's eternal wisdom and love. Forgiven and reconciled, be faithful to the Baptism which you have received! Be witnesses to the Gospel! As active and responsible members of the Church, be disciples and witnesses of Jesus Christ who reveals the Father! And abide always in the unity of the Spirit who is the giver of life![68]

World Youth Days 1984-2008

1984 - Rome: St Peter's Square, Palm Sunday (15 April 1984). International youth meeting on the occasion of the Holy Year of the Redemption. The Pope presents and entrusts young people with the Cross (22 April 1984).

1985 - Rome: St Peter's Square - Palm Sunday (31 March 1985). International youth meeting on the occasion of International Youth Year. The Holy Father addresses an Apostolic Letter to the youth of the world (31 March 1985). He announces the institution of World Youth Day (20 December 1985)

1986 - 1st World Youth Day: Theme: "Always be prepared to make a defence to anyone who calls you to account for the hope that is in you" (1 *Pt* 3:15). Celebration (diocesan level): Palm Sunday (23 March 1986).

1987 - 2nd World Youth Day: Theme: "We ourselves have known and put our faith in God's love towards ourselves" (1 *Jn* 4:16). Celebration (international level): Buenos Aires, Argentina (11-12 April 1987).

1988 - 3rd World Youth Day: Theme: "Do whatever he tells you" (*Jn* 2:5). Celebration (diocesan level): Palm Sunday (27 March 1988).

1989 - 4th World Youth Day: Theme: "I am the Way, the Truth and the Life" (*Jn* 14:6). Celebration (international level): Santiago de Compostela, Spain (15-20 August 1989).

1990 - 5th World Youth Day: Theme: "I am the vine, you are the branches" (*Jn* 15:5). Celebration (diocesan level): Palm Sunday (8 April 1990).

1991 - 6th World Youth Day: Theme: "You have received a spirit of sonship" (*Rm* 8:15). Celebration (international level): Czestochowa, Poland (10-15 August 1991).

1992 - 7th World Youth Day: Theme: "Go into all the world and preach the Gospel" (*Mk* 16:15). Celebration (diocesan level): Palm Sunday (12 April 1992).

1993 - 8th World Youth Day: Theme: "I came that they might have life, and have it to the full" (*Jn* 10:10). Celebration (international level): Denver, USA (10-15 August 1993).

1994 - 9th World Youth Day: Theme: "As the Father sent me, so am I sending you" (*Jn* 20:21). Celebration (diocesan level): Palm Sunday (27 March 1994).

1995 - 10th World Youth Day: Theme: "As the Father sent me, so am I sending you" (*Jn* 20:21). Celebration (international level): Manila, Philippines (10-15 January 1995).

1996 - 11th World Youth Day: Theme: "Lord, to whom shall we go? You have the words of eternal life" (*Jn* 6:68). Celebration (diocesan level): Palm Sunday (31 March 1996).

1997 - 12th World Youth Day: Theme: "Teacher, where are you staying? Come and see" (cf. *Jn* 1:38-39). Celebration (international level): Paris, France (19-24 August 1997).

1998 - 13th World Youth Day: Theme: "The Holy Spirit will teach you all things" (cf *Jn* 14:26). Celebration (diocesan level): Palm Sunday (5 April 1998).

1999 - 14th World Youth Day: Theme: "The Father loves you" (cf. *Jn* 16:27). Celebration (diocesan level): Palm Sunday (28 March 1999).

2000 - 15th World Youth Day - Youth Jubilee: Theme: "The Word became flesh and dwelt among us" (*Jn* 1:14). Celebration (international level): Rome, Italy (15-20 August 2000).

2001 - 16th World Youth Day: Theme: "If any want to become my followers, let them deny themselves and take up their cross daily and follow me" (*Lk* 9:23). Celebration (diocesan level): Palm Sunday (8 April).

2002 - 17th World Youth Day: Theme: "You are the salt of the earth ... you are the light of the world" (*Mt* 5:13, 14). Celebration (international level): Toronto, Canada (23-28 July 2002).

2003 - 18th World Youth Day: Theme: "Behold, your mother!" (*Jn* 19, 27). Celebration (diocesan level): Palm Sunday (13 April).

2004 - 19th World Youth Day: Theme: "We wish to see Jesus" (*Jn* 12, 21). Celebration (diocesan level): Palm Sunday (4 April).

2005 - 20th World Youth Day: Theme: "We have come to worship Him" (*Mt* 2, 2). International celebration: Cologne (August 16-21).

2006 - 21st World Youth Day: Theme: "Your word is a lamp to my feet and a light to my path" (*Ps* 119, 105). Celebration (diocesan level): Palm Sunday (9 April).

2007 - 22nd World Youth Day: Theme: "Just as I have loved you, you also should love one another" (*Jn* 13, 34). Celebration (diocesan level): Palm Sunday (8 April).

2008 - 23rd World Youth Day: Theme: "You will receive power when the Holy Spirit has come upon you; and you will be my witnesses" (*Ac* 1, 8). International celebration - Sydney, 15-20 July 2008.

Endnotes

[1] St Catherine of Siena, Letter 368.
[2] Tor Vergata 2000, 15th WYD John Paul II.
[3] 23rd WYD is to be celebrated 15-20 July 2008, Sydney, Australia.
[4] Sydney 2008, invitation to 23rd WYD, Benedict XVI.
[5] Santiago de Compostela 1989, 4th WYD, John Paul II.
[6] Denver 1993, 8th WYD, John Paul II.
[7] Philippines 1995, 10th WYD, John Paul II.
[8] Tor Vergata 2000, 15th WYD John Paul II.
[9] Toronto 2002, 17th WYD, John Paul II.
[10] Tor Vergata 2000, 15th WYD John Paul II.
[11] Cologne 2005, 20th WYD , Benedict XVI.
[12] Sydney 2008, invitation to 23rd WYD, Benedict XVI.
[13] Santiago de Compostela 1989, 4th WYD, John Paul II.
[14] Denver 1993, 8th WYD, John Paul II.
[15] Philippines 1995, 10th WYD, John Paul II.
[16] Santiago de Compostela 1989, 4th WYD, John Paul II.
[17] Paris 1997, 12th WYD, John Paul II.
[18] Santiago de Compostela 1989, 4th WYD, John Paul II.
[19] Santiago de Compostela 1989, 4th WYD, John Paul II.
[20] Toronto 2002, 17th WYD, John Paul II.
[21] Denver 1993, 8th WYD, John Paul II.
[22] Santiago de Compostela 1989, 4th WYD, John Paul II.
[23] Philippines 1995, 10th WYD, John Paul II.
[24] Philippines 1995, 10th WYD, John Paul II.
[25] Paris 1997, 12th WYD, John Paul II.
[26] Paris 1997, 12th WYD, John Paul II.
[27] Tor Vergata 2000, 15th WYD John Paul II.
[28] Toronto 2002, 17th WYD, John Paul II.
[29] Paris 1997, 12th WYD, John Paul II.
[30] Sydney 2008, invitation to 23rd WYD, Benedict XVI.
[31] Paris 1997, 12th WYD, John Paul II.
[32] Tor Vergata 2000, 15th WYD John Paul II.
[33] Tor Vergata 2000, 15th WYD John Paul II.

[34] Tor Vergata 2000, 15th WYD John Paul II.
[35] Cologne 2005, 20th WYD, Benedict XVI.
[36] Cologne 2005, 20th WYD, Benedict XVI.
[37] Sydney 2008, invitation to 23rd WYD, Benedict XVI.
[38] Santiago de Compostela 1989, 4th WYD, John Paul II.
[39] Santiago de Compostela 1989, 4th WYD, John Paul II.
[40] Tor Vergata 2000, 15th WYD John Paul II.
[41] Santiago de Compostela 1989, 4th WYD, John Paul II.
[42] Santiago de Compostela 1989, 4th WYD, John Paul II.
[43] Sydney 2008, invitation to 23rd WYD, Benedict XVI.
[44] Sydney 2008, invitation to 23rd WYD, Benedict XVI.
[45] Sydney 2008, invitation to 23rd WYD, Benedict XVI.
[46] Sydney 2008, invitation to 23rd WYD, Benedict XVI.
[47] Denver 1993, 8th WYD, John Paul II.
[48] Philippines 1995, 10th WYD, John Paul II.
[49] Santiago de Compostela 1989, 4th WYD, John Paul II.
[50] Santiago de Compostela 1989, 4th WYD, John Paul II.
[51] Santiago de Compostela 1989, 4th WYD, John Paul II.
[52] Santiago de Compostela 1989, 4th WYD, John Paul II.
[53] Denver 1993, 8th WYD, John Paul II.
[54] Denver 1993, 8th WYD, John Paul II.
[55] Denver 1993, 8th WYD, John Paul II.
[56] Philippines 1995, 10th WYD, John Paul II.
[57] Philippines 1995, 10th WYD, John Paul II.
[58] Santiago de Compostela 1989, 4th WYD, John Paul II.
[59] Santiago de Compostela 1989, 4th WYD, John Paul II.
[60] Santiago de Compostela 1989, 4th WYD, John Paul II.
[61] Denver 1993, 8th WYD, John Paul II.
[62] Denver 1993, 8th WYD, John Paul II.
[63] Philippines 1995, 10th WYD, John Paul II.
[64] Cologne 2005, 20th WYD, Benedict XVI.
[65] Toronto 2002, 17th WYD, John Paul II.
[66] Toronto 2002, 17th WYD, John Paul II.
[67] Santiago de Compostela 1989, 4th WYD, John Paul II.
[68] Paris 1997, 12th WYD, John Paul II.

A Way of Life for Young Catholics

Written for young Catholics who want to live their faith more deeply but are not sure what steps to take, this booklet contains practical, down-to-earth advice on many aspects of daily life, whether spiritual ('Prayer', 'Confession') or moral ('Alcohol and drugs', 'Dating and chastity') or emotional ('Coping with worry or suffering') or vocational ('Discovering my vocation', 'Finding a good husband or wife'). It will be especially helpful for older confirmation candidates, students, and young adults hoping to learn more about their faith.

Fr Stephen Wang, a priest in the Diocese of Westminster, has worked in parish ministry, a university chaplaincy, and giving retreats for young people. He now teaches philosophy, theology, and pastoral studies at Allen Hall Seminary in London.

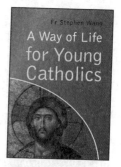

ISBN: 978 1 86082 487 6

CTS Code: Do 774

Open wide the doors for Christ

This collection of prayers, meditations and writings of John Paul II is intended primarily for personal reflection and inspiration. As one of the most edifying and eloquent popes of all time, John Paul II addressed a panoply of universal and intensely personal concerns. These thought provoking excerpts on love, hope, discipleship, forgiveness, suffering, sickness and old age, work, prayer, and the Eucharist proclaim above all, the love and hope of Christ risen. They provide a helpful introduction to the depth and breadth of Christianity itself, by one of its most articulate advocates.

ISBN: 1 86082 366 X

CTS Code: D 674

Informative Catholic Reading

We hope that you have enjoyed reading this booklet.

If you would like to find out more about CTS booklets - we'll send you our free information pack and catalogue.

Please send us your details:

Name ....

Address ....

....

....

Postcode ....

Telephone ....

Email ....

Send to: CTS, 40-46 Harleyford Road,
Vauxhall, London
SE11 5AY

Tel: 020 7640 0042
Fax: 020 7640 0046
Email: info@cts-online.org.uk